D1546232

CAMERA

CAMERA

MAXINE CHERNOFF

SUBITO PRESS 2017

Camera © 2017 Maxine Chernoff
All rights reserved.

ISBN: 978-0-9988594-3-9

Design & typesetting by HR Hegnauer
    www.hrhegnauer.com
Cover photograph by Emilian Chirila
Text typeset in Garamond

Subito Press
Department of English
University of Colorado at Boulder
226 UCB
Boulder, CO 80309-0226
subitopress.org

Distributed by Small Press Distribution
1341 Seventh Street
Berkeley, California 94710
spdbooks.org

Generous funding for this publication has been provided by the Creative
Writing Program in the Department of English and the Innovative Seed
Grant Program at the University of Colorado at Boulder.

CONTENTS

Preface

(2:45 pm. 20 January 2014)

Lord, increase my bewilderment.

Fanny Howe

The work of this moment: a life is celebrated and others are born and die as I write this sentence. There is the small hum of a machine that runs on the melted bones of dinosaurs and the smell of cut vegetation. There is the taste of salt on my knuckle and glaciers melting and fires in the south of my state. There are circumstances. There are feelings. There are connections to be made or not about memes and twerks and a YouTube version of Johnny Cash at San Quentin when all the prisoners were white. The work lives now and in retrospect. The work lives in an empire of great cruelty and wealth, where the average citizen is punished daily and not given what she needs—(give us this day our gluten-free bread). Drones hit targets as we speak. The last bee in the garden has its singular existence as it approaches the lily and is part of a community whose existence is threatened by a plague and pesticides, and yet it cannot present its own case to the world: hence, Emily Dickinson. That is the work, giving voice to itself, holding within itself the deep notions of the moment. The poem's attention is also its ignorance. The work is beyond unkind to everything it omits. The work cannot fulfill its duties of repairing the broken world all around it. The work struggles to contain itself. It does not bleed to death or get crushed by an army. The poem sucks the nectar and returns to its hive.

Nest

Always the quaking of relief.

John Ashbery

In a swamp the mangroves shade
the nest of eggs blue as
your eyes, who know the century's
sorrow as light knows the drift of
a feather through turbulent air.

You whose vows evaporate
like mist from an ocean
where starfish and algae feel
the touch of an invisible poison
in water's slow retreat of grace,
and blueness is reflection
of a steepled, latticed sky.

Trellised world, which pleads
in low tones for a window
where ledgers fill
with threads and feathers of
birds, whose beaks crush
certain berries in their ripeness,
this small economy of need.

Drift

And though we are not celestial bodies,
our hearts there do aspire.

Claudia Keelan

To swim in the eye and rest
in the beak of that bird whose throat
is midnight under the spruce you
planted from the seeds of the dark angel,
whose presence is the smoothness
of forgetting or the wind-tossed
feather of letting go

To be the cathedral of reason
that grows as in summer
when Daphne produces
a single twig, leaves silvered.

To wish what is lost be restored
in the house of blue beads where
light is fractured and reworked
to resemble a violin in a rainstorm.

How we shape wires and strings
and lace into terms of request
and make a pact to endure this heat.

How we are lifted to a sky
full of cottonwood seeds,
archipelago of sight glistening at noon.

Fossil

Soul and signature

conceived of egg and feather.

Nothing liquid or envious of

flight: orphan sundered from

narrative's how and why.

Where you stand,

no solidity for lamp light or

summer's late full moon.

You register the hardness

of stone, the solid geometry

of words. No fleeting allegory

to hold you, form a circle

of want, enclosing space.

Semblance

In its qualities a drop of rain is like the Nile.

Mahmud Shabistari

A crow tends a branch
on meaning's tree, where
a single word's limit,
meets trouble's dark road,
deadpan map, stolid
as Keaton's face. The story
swells and grows motives,
as weeds disguise gardens
in summer's amplitude.
Nothing undoes day's dazed
grace unless it is captioned
or chiseled, here where your
whisper encounters
the ghost of witness, as a glass
that holds water's history.

Moonlit

When I fall asleep, your eyes close.

Pablo Neruda

Place love first in the botany of days,
trumpet vines reaching, nascent
songs in caverned throats.
The chorus holds a branch
as love its own economies,
and as wings lift words,
a feather floats on air, above
earth's dark landing.

Stratagem of descent, turning
eyes closed, doubled wholeness,
raspy whisper in the ear
of a saint, faint tick
of a small star escaping
its orthodoxy. Never had
such luster shared a name
with limits. Gathered and stripped,
culled from objects strange
as books that ring like bells,
here and here, actor and witness
to regions' cold restraint.

Argument

Its feathers

laced to

breath of sky

and molecule,

blasphemy and rapture,

the berry its

beak holds in

abeyance of hunger,

no issue,

the branch

no harangue,

the berry and branch,

the call and response,

the material

world holds

issue, no issue.

Corona

Purple crown of release
as stories become the said.
Narrative of hands,
subplot of eyes' brief
notion of flags in a sky
of launchings. Comic
relief of a vertical feather
in sand, a button undone,
lips upturned in wanting.

Be not long at the joust,
Love. Carry my hankie,
riding past on your memory
horse, its dull armor clanking.
Endings arrive as seasons:
the peony sheds in the wind,
its ripeness our carpet.

Findings

For all flesh is as grass.

1.

Laced roots tease an opening when tendrils

        break through sleep, unfurl another spring,

in sluices and hidden stones covered

        by earth's dusty glove: language's lost home,

how one word

        settles, another dies,

          twined,

        with slow offering, woven as

passage.

2.

A cape of rain, season's slow reply

      falls on lips, words chipped, a canopy

of salt-filled sky, eyes wander,

      grass gives way and words bend earth,

sky's whiteness capping afternoon.

3.

thigh of hill

breast of leaves

belly of witness.

    Wind takes pollen

           and dusky loam

hides turtle shells,

mouse ears,

the smallest fleck of bone.

    Late frost issues summons

to blossom-death, lost fruit falling.

4.

Olive trees ancient as time's increase,

a subtle force

           subtracts our burden.

Eyes close on the scene a world

    can't witness.

5.

   Unmasked in trees,

hollow owl, burden blossomed

enact their comedy in time:

            lines rippling in space:

hands fill with color, hiding in

      the iridescence: green of wings.

6.

   Under skies
in the marrow and sound
      of chambers closing in the leaves,
      there is a silence
                  resplendent as ice.

   No words say you are not
      alone on   the small shoals
            of belief.

7.

Hemmed instincts crack the space

shoal laden

with earth and time's increase:

      geography fulfilled by clavicle

and breast. Bridge of

          spine the whispered

path, river in the ear makes

present what is chastened,

          loved, discarded.

8.

To leave behind remnant or nest,

    dear amulet of bird-tossed air, pungent

with rain, a galleon cloud tossed

               expressing a limit

               it cannot cross.

               His box of owls

    at the impasse of borders.

Her body a home to his wanderings.

9.

To quote the oyster: signature in words

      worn down like fissured rain. Finding

things mute, we speak volumes.

          Finding things broken,

we suture them with phrases.

            She knits him a body. Her

      fingers spell words on his eyelids.

Event

An event must in some way end before its
narration can begin.

Christian Metz

Then doves and the thrush and the late
afternoon of the swallows under the bridge and
the fathoms of sleep and then the hollows of
dialogue aspiring to contain the rich facts
of what didn't happen when it seemed to have,
and then a disquisition on the luster of windows
in the morning when a psalm is read
before lightning strikes the spire of a tall church
in the city of your birth, and then centuries
of robes of saffron or black and vespers or prayer
on cold granite or at a wall where guards
stand with AK-47s and ghosts witness their attempts
with sorrow, unlike human sorrow, which is a stream
that evaporates when language interrupts its flow.
And the ministry of a quiet voice when what
is needed is a bell or a glass filled to a certain
level and made to vibrate with a spoon, and before
this ending another ending and after that another
and no agreement between parties as to whether
the story is over or this is a respite between
exhaustion and pleading. And the irises shallowly
covered in dirt, emerge purple in spring,
world without end, as words are endless,
sending their tendrils towards the next refrain.

Gaze

The earliest pilgrims shared a cathedral for a heart.

Jeanette Winterson

To be the camera for your gaze,
I made myself a candle and a view,
a wish and furtive trees just to the right.
The window, dressed in black, was lifted
like a carpet toward the sky, and feathers
blinked and swarmed around a body meant
to signal flight. The house arrayed for
mourning was too full of ghosts and glass
to feel the ancient history of floorboards'
prelude and retreat. Harsh light filled
the closet with misgivings. Absent
of words, pages were relief from hasty,
moonlit vows. The world, once beaded
with desire, was pale milk-white.
Paper moths were thrown into the fray.

Camera

*Unlike memory, photos do not themselves
preserve meaning.*

John Berger

You exit camera's gaze,
through the aperture,
politics unknown,
motives shrouded in leaves,
certain as any tomb.
Without limit or attitude
luster is mechanical,
grows reasons
melting in summer's heat.
Hope is a vessel of
longitude's practice,
lengthening space
as glasses toast
skin's translucence
in a photo you took
when the story found
its way home to the mind
of its choosing.
A dreamed equation
suffices for essence,
being stretched over
a candle's swift burning.
Grief is a body of fire spreading
in the branches of a landscape
painted and patiently framed.

Air

I lifted to mind a piece of bright blue air.

The stare of others as thoughts hide matters
and dust recedes as a movie in reverse.
So much subtracted and fractioned
by the grain or issue of an eye.
One an echo, another a star—
meaning floats like a hat
suspended from shiny strings.
In the shallow, hedgy grove,
birds hide among briny reeds
where midnight outlasts small
altars and obsessions.
What names our histories of mud
and sand and the dim, curled shadow
we see crouched near the door?
Globe of radiant heat witnesses our mishaps
and mistakes, our answers and our bells.

Sleep

*Even the most fragmentary shot still represents
a complete segment of reality.*

Christian Metz

Without a lens, blind
to the world's progress,
its whorls and notches
and silent omissions,
what stood in the sun
when the sky was
a bowl and a wish.
You touch your own
desires, as vines twine
up ancient walls, part
of a tale you once told
at midnight when
tender shoots broke
through soil and roots white
as parchment reached deeper
into earth's invisible book.
A directionless juncture,
where birds swoop and clouds
alight, and hands weave words.
A shard and a pebble,
a rope and a plan, spoken as
half-truths, escaping
the "o" of your mouth.

Afternoon

All one retains of a film is its plot and a few images.

Christian Metz

Their shadows carved in snow,
ghosts wander in eternity,
their habit of existence
escaping our cognition
until we surrender
light and location,
dried bark and dead leaves,
decayed in their mystery
no more than summer's cloth
lowered in the garden
with its flowers behind
flowers. Lost on the screen
is the morning he said
this and you that and
the future hummed in the bushes
like a slow, windowless fire.
We haunt the world looking
for ourselves, the ones
who know the soft antler-buds
of deer. We forget the scene
in the room of the said
where curtains and bed and light,
latticed as lace, made your face
unfamiliar, mine too shrouded
in layers of hope, which is,
as gauze, a semblance

of our hiding. As we opened
to the other, beyond seasons
and borders, the world,
with everything in place, held
small truths untold by any voice.
A vista and a ledge, custom and dust
of living, spread. Our story obscure,
the room shuttered, the lateness
of the day a swift descent.
You said a word that filled
a momentary gap, lacing the world
in tangled sound and string.

Emblem

In a film a house would be a shot of a staircase.

Christian Metz

The chambered air
remembered—
surgical, smooth,
until location itself
seemed an invention
of will. The house,
particular to our longings,
its blue light dimming
then returning
to the story every morning.
With no name
for love's statuary
its swans and ready doves,
its trees awaiting
clarification, objects
drifted until we recovered
the ancient art
of listening as we
spoke our names
in a new language
occasioned by desire.

Scene

The cinema is a specific language.

Christian Metz

What the body might guess,
what the hand requests,
what language assumes
becomes amulet,
which is to say
I am carrying your face
in a locket in a box
to a virtual location
guarded by kestrels,
suggesting the scene's
geography of love and dirt,
trees smeared by darkness
and bones' white luster.
In the moonlit blue house,
where snow won't fall
unless called upon,
grace enters as requested,
lands next to you, grasped,
as if love were reflex,
simple as weather.

Granted

A film is always like a book and not like a conversation.

Christian Metz

As I saw your face nearing
my face, snow fell through
a keyhole and opened the door.
We went inside and watched
windows wax green and gold.
Spring, we decided, was more
oppressive than winter with its alyssum
and clover and the sheer weight of life
crowding us off the page.
We stayed in bed for years
and took our cures patiently
from each other's cups.
We read *Bleak House* and
stored our money in socks.
Nothing opened as we did.

Invisible

Stillness is life.

Dust-mote world, whirled
with time's
constraints as minions
nodding at antiphony.

Inference flies
out the window:
Grief's companion
Loss is streamed
in live with bees.

Under a canopy
of spring a bridge
of armatures remains,
winter's dross and
high avowals fancied
as a system of roots,
fever played
as a deadpan motif.

If stamps were chalked
and signs read small or
mistakable, what
would measure task's location?

Throw me where light
waves as a star blown
through a brown night
of constraints.

Let the viewer
Assert his needs,
prickly as want
or self-effacement,
unseen as a rag on
the ocean floor.

The Possible

The stationary blasts of waterfalls.

Wordsworth

The moss-covered birds I clean
in the stream look at me clearly.

A baby floats by: Moses?—I am
texting you when the dream concludes.

So much to tend, oneself included,
liminal clouds leaking cold rain.

Location as anchor and ivy-filled
absence: the spoken as dirt's surest witness.

Awake to subtractions, seasons of smoke,
Aleppo's horizons drop from the sky.

Your private museum contains this world,
which doesn't make sense, unless in a photo,

but no—it is here, where silk worms
tend it: a milk-colored shroud cloaking its wounds.

Remembered

for D.F.

A nameless place

is conjured by a flow

of words until its source

is filled with expectation

as cameras hold the hour,

opaque and filled with loss,

until the watch is over

and someone speaks

in daytime's somber light

what slips into our grief.

We beg the hours

to encumber the location

where, eyes closed,

we've come to stand

above these mossy stones.

Future

Forbidden flowers and herbs/are history's foodstuff.

Old snow falls on this poem
about the past, our lives
remembered, as funerals
by those who never attend but
imagine the slender coffin,
the sheen of its bright handles.
There, on the dark lawn, you
meet your former self
asking a lover to step aside
as memory impinges on
an invitation to dance.
The next scene comes unbidden
as an outbreak of disease: there
he stands with his eyes mercurial;
there she weeps at her rendition
of their sorrow. Snow falls on them
both, laden with reasons and candles,
and in the corner a table is set
where your former self shares
its dinner with one
you have become. The radiant
fruit you share has gotten
overripe, waiting for its season.

Day Book

Give your acting the progression of
one-thing-after-another.

Bertolt Brecht

This game of resemblance,
this skein of intention: wool-
gathered words
spin a way through.

A trickle of sunlight
marks afternoon's presence.
Where you stand is location,
story the frame, meaning,
the smoke that slips
under the door. St. Peter's bells, a
wren at the window, cloister of
birds in the lofty stone pine.

Then you are here, love,
your face in the view. Aperture
open to day's random practice, the
usual framing of subject and
moment: hint of occurrence,
shudder of cloud.

To Live on Air

Black is a bright light on a dark day.

Bill Viola

Wholeness reckoned
as a stream,
beauty tossed
as scarves
at a bazaar,
the meal never served
as want becomes
the cellos
in the piece, music
emanating
from two griefs.
Sighted and recited
words repeat
their vow to live

on air, ashen as leaves
under a log
or faces in a photo
speaking as if meshed
in half-lit vows.

As night prepares
its jewels, the play
begins when
Prospero works his
charms, by which
a world appears.

Notion

A place where the visible is discontinuous.

John Berger

The lunar sublime,
whose berries, dispersed
by winds' distant ledger,
tell of the slumber
of bees swallowed in sun's
ripe task, location and
calling, destined,
as bright delay marks
increase and issue.

On that shore you were dying,
erased by rustling in the dream-leaves,
as the nest in the rushes is
looted by a brief red notion.
On what earth did we measure
the deluged choirs? Whose eye
witnessed our landings, as if
chased from pretense? Whose
bright launchings drifted over
our empty hands?

Curtain

In rooms of sleep
your silent witness
is a glove, blue with
density as a summer lake.
On a light- speckled landing,
you turn to observe
the view but finds a gap
that isn't as much
window as bent mirror.
Prophetic curtains
enchant the absence
with a vocal breeze,
notion of a plan.
What you thought
a fault line
removes the capable
earth and blisters
your desires. An orb
of sleep lifts you
before a flood of rushing
error sweeps the
the scene. Complacent
and composed
you carve a perfect window,
light arriving at
the hour of its framing.

As If

if loved--could change the weather, could send aspen through rooftops and make rain, make shiny petals spin, change matter to attention. Plants blink and stars send energy toward the lonely billions, who, if loved, love as no others, love as themselves in patterns of tongue and lips, if loved send roots, send arms, send the tumbling grace of notes, if loved send grasses from brackish water toward salty air, send, if loved, attention, send, the brassy strings of noble firs and the harmonies of roots maintaining ground: all possible gatherings spring from the eye, the hand, the blessed words of vapor and truth. The hummingbird asks the flower the hour of closing, not a grief but if loved a testing.

Did I Tell You?

The Kansas City Stomp was not written in Kansas City.

Jelly Roll Morton

How you were made of words on a lazy Sunday when letters hovered, birds against winter's white. On the borders of a page the indifferent field was absent of decorative stone, how you were an expenditure of voice and stranger still, said nothing. Born of time and its corrections, memory's trap-door, the song is a limit, the smallest bridge to the next hesitation.

Ballad

An ethereal wind chorus opens the second scene.

Stanley Sadie

Recumbent this October without fog, without robes of silk tied across the sky, the white of wings is stranger to this air. The sanctity of an hour is crystalline response, as we place our kindest selves in the world, which wears our sorrow as a lover the scent of her beloved. How we wrest distance from its map to reach the radiance of late flowers, funereal in color, ordinary as containment. Place me in the earth, and I will breathe for days. Lock the doors to the actual and the world will mime its calm retreat into dusky grapes and glistening bell.

Later

We have been living in this same moment
ever since we were conceived.

Bill Viola

1.

Shadowed and screened,
your place in the setting
is morning's task.
You ask the cortex
to light upon a fly's buzzing
as interruption in the song
of recurrence. In a room
of simplifications, figure
and ground mark disclosure,
the shapes at the window
a way of knowing.
Any clear pane reflects
sight and inclination.
You stand witnessing
the world's traffic,
shaping tree and declension.

2.

Sing as if heaven
still fits in the plan,
partial story made whole,
woman and man.
The bowing trees,
as felt in a song
by Nina Simone,
whose deep voice
knows a storm can fit
inside a shadowed box.

Pilgrim

Give praise with the rippling speech.

Anne Porter

A green pilgrim, reaching beyond the fence, as words
fill with sounds that can't be uttered, and children are
lost in a forest where trees' thickness impenetrable as
light cannot assist their tactics of escape.

You offer prayers in a vacant store, no higher being or lower
remedy holds dear what is not said. The dark winter twigs are
portents, birds, motives.

You are found in the gloaming, encountering stranger plots,
twisted truths, a face you love stripped by some grief. Grief
too a tendril reaching its soft feathers
toward the branch,
its bitter wants held tightly as the world.

Calendar

All this mental glass.

Muted and thinned, register blank as November
when the sun lends its approval and rainwater
glistens with arrival: no cure in your hand,
holding this day as a gathering of string.

Wandering with his words, a voice erases meaning.
All crescendo now, as leaves with their usual fanfare
crush ants retreating to dark earth and industry.
We wait in line amid its outlaws, mutinies,
and rebel chords, making hunger artists of our needs.

The crudely built gate marks limits and treasons. Ask again if
This is making sense. Quote the man in the barrel.
Whose ripe world waits for slow arrival?

Totem

If the stars then the running
if the grain then the taking
under stealth and erasure
reprobate until closure if
words then horizon
suffice to say bodies
leeward when rising
then faces frame
layer if wanting
then touch
if vacant then nascent if
sinking
then leaf-lined
the kneeling then grass if
whispered to others
then children count
ships a flotilla
of swan
if flotilla of meaning
then relations to squander if
the whole and
if closure
then voices
the breaking
if leaves
sign a locus
then ready and sentient

Edge

Runaway thought, I wanted to write it; instead,
I write that it has run away.

Pascal

Not the day for the false alarm,
the robin-breasted moment,
the double entendre in the mirror.
How can we know, given your worried
eyes and surrogacy of words?
Go with your clothes tucked
in a sack, your jewels hidden in sand,
your stale loaf that once smelled of creation.
What hammers you into a shape
is blunt and uninformed.
Hit or miss, our course of hours,
planet carrying its load of stones,
tissues and small green notions.
Eyes closed to the view, you listen to
your thoughts spin lace. What you don't see
evaporates with the next cold breeze,
the next harm, positioned to descend
when least expected. What we endure
is our story. Words, abjured, are
a forest floor, thick with patterns,
left for seasons to bury as the dead
we know so well their breath is
outline and cold witness.

To Own

The shot is an actual unit.

Christian Metz

The blistering shore whose cliffs spawn
birds among the ruins of olive trees;
tethered there, the hosts whose language
makes them strange and bartered,
as life evolves around a plague-filled
site we've come to call not ours.

The news is filled with one true plot,
that men make war and trouble stands
to view the scene, the boss orders
workers to make jackets bombs or pies.

Whose ghost will take the blame for all
the dying in the leaves, what world
kills seeds and makes the bees lose
their high season thick with industry?

Cue the stinging rupture which we take to mean
a death has been inscribed upon the day
we crush the grapes and say the prayer,
which still is offered for a reason split, a rift
between this ledge and that.

Here is the cortege, holding meaning in its hands,
the barest omens dense as bulbs we plant
in fall. Seasons travel in the world of pure design,
their blooming too a death though
for the moment decorated as a bride.

Staircase

The body

launched in time's

descent

from attitude

to state

of being

when rushed air

leaves the mouth

and breath

is dumb.

White light

obscures the shape

of thought

an act of faith

to clutch the hand

that fails to hold

the sheerest

thread

of now to there.

Emergent

Sumptuous destitution.

Like wasps
stinging in the unkind world
where love is stretched
and painted green.
The dumb world gleaming
like bells from a tower
in a painting of a valley,
where a single puff of smoke
translates the scene.
Where to travel
on the empty train?

To sonify a spinoff,
to spin a pearl
until its oyster closes
on resistance, until
its drift finds a ready
landing in dark water,
submerging to a place
beyond eyes and the soft
underpinning of words.

In spring you want more,
the pale leaf's beckoning,
the heart's easy notice.
Sky and belief part ways.
The crisp, unseeming world
readies for the task.
Tell it something
it can believe.

Location

After his death she dreams of roses and bones.

Anne Carson

Under an alphabet of clouds,
earth's sweet breviary.
We launch paper boats
in afternoon's penumbra.

Skilled at turning as elephants
that feel the cold bones. Fumbling
leaves on their junket to nowhere
have their place in the story
of days' circumference.

When you leave, the grass will cover
my eyes. And under my eyelids,
dark orchids and wild grapes
climbing. The air will stir in its shroud.

Plan

And Charon,

in its dark orbit,

light-years distant

from the improvisatory

dance, the momentary

lapse of rain, on earth's

unsettled ground.

In the news

a flag is taken down.

Let us make a flag, love.

Let it fly on Pluto's constant moon.

Between

Angel and puppet. Now we will have a play.

Rilke

Stately in your ermine coat or naked
as a fish in his glassy underworld,
you do not ask for love, as if it were only
meant for midnight dreams of peopled worlds
in bustling rooms, their features bright as candy
or dark as moss by a northern gate.
What you hold dear becomes your task
as buds open like allegories of lips.
Let the play begin with the theater
empty and only chairs as witness.

Noli mi tangere

Go thou to Rome—at once the Paradise,
The grave, the city, and the wilderness.

Shelley

You find it there and pick it up,
lost already in the language

• • •

Near Garibaldi's monument, blue blisters its limit.
Untangled clouds gather: proper nouns amass.
Try to keep it real meets the ancient
stone pine: all lenses point to Rome

• • •

First they came for the architecture:
harsh sun is closer here. Placards
mark the rift, sacked and burned
(just as today)(Aleppo) (Mosul) (Bamiyan) (..

• • •

Of Keats' grave, Shelley writes:
"...an open space among the ruins
covered in winter in violets and daisies,"
his own near the top
of the outsiders' cemetery

• • •

Too tired to wear the earbuds
for the film, every moment
I observed was captured on his face,
as if saying, I am here

•   •   •

never sorry you exist
never say that, love

•   •   •

Hölderlin saw the rift in the sky

Black moon means hidden

He got a kill fee

She took her leave

Literally and also not

•   •   •

In what ways have I lost you?

•   •   •

Say your treasons are legendary.
You trespass on the world,
its soil leaking remedies. You take
the sacred root and gnash it
in your hand, fingers yellowing. This
is not your world. Take your hand
and touch the stone. It is a stone.
Above the outsiders' cemetery,
a shirtless man tends his geranium.
Memento Mori with Peroni.

• • •

(How we didn't go to Rome and slept alone for years

• • •

I visited her in her dying. She asked for a poem, which terrified
me
more than her dying. I wanted to take her up and somehow save
her.
No words for that
—all the rye we drank later to forget.

• • •

twigs on the street form a lantern:

then a leaf's interruption

• • •

May you find the form to enclose you:
like the sycamore in its window,
leaves disrupted by the starlings,
black eminence backgrounding sun,
twice seen in the pane

• • •

As stories have two views.
Remember that, partisans,
as clouds shift from Dalmatian
to palomino. There
is always more to tell

• • •

(Re disruption, what scene had you in mind? Get back to me,
please

• • •

For I exist to see you
in your perfect rags and wounds.

• • •

What we lose we keep:
lavender sky at 6:02
Partial column on a hill.
The news as it flickers
out like a star

• • •

Tourists everywhere (I among them).
Voices at the catacombs: those who came
for The Grand Tour or in order
to save their lives
(Keats on his final green bed

•   •   •

The supplicants arrive, blessing
the possible cure. Candles lit.
Coins tossed. As many hospitals
as churches peer out from the ruins.

•   •   •

Chosen at 6 years, most served 30.
If they broke their vows, the vestal virgins
were buried live at Colline Gate,
past which the bus travels daily
(here I am).
Food and water for several days
because they could not technically
be harmed: consenting to their deaths,
proper maidens still

•   •   •

Full of affection and uncertainty,
you are a galleon of flesh. You sail
on the Tiber under the many bridges,
past the junction where cattle barges
arrived to market three millennia ago

•   •   •

The sacrifice of living is to see:
So much invisibility, how the missing
among us measure their days by color
of the sky, whispering whom
they love, dear faces all, as charms

• • •

Pristine among the ruins, the small
temple to Caesar. Perfect in its roundness.
Everything coherent once, discrete
as that bush where sparrows practice
divination by gathering crumbs:
I divine my love, his lips,
his voice in my ear, my eyes his

• • •

The cloister where nuns pray,
demolished and then rebuilt.
Enduring through devotion.

• • •

Alessandro the taxi driver
tells me about the Nobel Prize.
"Bob Dee-lan, musica. Genio."

• • •

Rain's particular measure is voiceover
for the day. History rewriting its future
in the innocent eyes of saints.
Saint Kafka of Prague

• • •

Find a vacant corner where
the light gives off
some warmth,
all the piety you'll need

• • •

You slept too late and love the day,
from macadam to frescoed ceiling.
San Luigi De Francesco's dark corner
of Caravaggios--filled with agony
and light, the human scales

• • •

Our bodies are smaller
than the head of Juno &
suffer more than representation
can depict: here is the bust
of Goethe: marble's equanimity.

• • •

and yet to say it all is not enough:
your shadow cast on the Tiber:
the fleet passing of your chance,
witnessed and enacted.
This too is not the sum:

•   •   •

when you leave others
will arrive to bless the air.

Told

But that's another story.

Ray Ragosta

Here stands Jules
without his Jim, there
an old man weeping
for his wild fruit.
An innocent daughter
has gone to the woods
where the story encloses
her ultimate day. You hold
a spoon, its glacier
of salt, a loaf of bread,
its mushroom cap top.
And he is with her
at the blue beach house
where only fables get told
in the dark. The heart too,
a book that nothing escapes,
not even the dust on the frontispiece
he won't read or the yarn
that was destined to be a hat.

Verb

The verb 'to be' is the most protean of the English language.

Grammar.com

A shoe unlaced could be our undoing,
safety an affectation, like an orchid resembling
a dragonfly, non-existence under
darkest lunar crease. Edges
move forward, seeking a tender obligation
fulfilled by one's hand. Tragic skin, thin
as paper, eyes as candles,
breath a museum. To be nothing
but light, seeking ourselves
on the Möbius strip of intention,
finding our grace but losing
our captioned ending, charming
ourselves into belief, which dims
in the future perfect, and got burned
in the past. We die for want, *the said*
a last bastion, waiting for history,
a music for stars basking in time's slow regress.

Story

Repeating is also naming.

William Gass

At the crossroads of notice, where stories wait ready
to meet their stunned donors, the ones who know
reasons like people the weather or names
of their children, the story's rough edges and
rotten boards leaning toward yesterday's songs of
embarking, the river whose bank
is covered in lilies for somebody's death though
no one is speaking. Coming to grief might
break the sheer boundaries and license the weeping
at rest under eaves of the lake-facing cottage.
The one who came asking goes home without closure,
the one with the story unfreezes the pen
and lets it drop under the porch one invents
as part of the scene, the window one makes
of scorched and spent redress, the people who wait
as though they are human, and words are their breathing.
Leave them there waiting until they are needed to wander
towards mention on plot's tuneless page. Awaiting an author,
they watch the moths landing, on time's hazy screen, where
everyone falters along with their reasons for silence
or speaking, the uncounted numbers awaiting their words.

Artifact

First the weighing then the grace then the reaching
toward design. A future artifact knows you well,
redacted zones of intimacy and ardor left for colder climes,
the green notion of branches rocked by wind and growth
stays whole by error, held in abeyance, reified or deified,
numbered. The story travels in the longitude of seldom seen
adumbrations, decoder rings, tea and letters from observers
of your absence. Whole or retracted, the night gloved our
hands. What did we feel holding the world wrapped in velvet?

One

*As she kisses him, the "Tristan chord" is outlined by
stopped horns and cellos.*

Barry Millington

An annunciation bled onto a frame
under lilac cover, night issued its
malfeasance, a bright name for error.

A word went home after staying up late, its
round vowels listing to the right
of a human abstract, articulated
as inoculation from grief.

Here is the first stage, not denial but treatise
on the unseemly love of water for air.

No telling how turning will right the brief
notion of disaster so close to our compass.

Misremembered

Into the darkness of someone else's garden.

Pushkin

Rain cast doubt on how it felt to touch your
cheek, small hollow of resemblance, its
shore, distinct, in half-lit stages of sleep.
Mostly not a tragedy that sheets were white
or blue, the hour too late or only later.

A pearl, its imperfections no more subtle than waves
that bent that tree, where it stood among
the overhanging, half-remembered boughs.

Let us not forget the moment in its vague dimensions
of retreat, both melody and scale. How we bask
in our forgetting, loosen notes from song.

Cuchulain

You wind up in limbo with liars and thieves who fear you, then sew your own shroud. The exit a portal: you must grow wings. And like crickets in season and crows at dawn, or the moss at your feet feeding the stream, you are small and of things, as if heaven or whatnot were the simple yard of a house in spring. Must you believe? In sewing, in patience, as vines cover the windows and you let them. Come in, you say, to the wind at the gate. You scatter your weakness, splayed on white sheets, no homecomings, hearth, or register. You mend what needs fixing, taking your cue from autumn's trick of divesting, here and not here at once.

Invention

Daylight disbanded the phantom crew.

Edith Wharton

A cottonwood seed left in its husk,
no question arched towards lucidity,
its quivers oil and water-worked.
How we land is called the drowning.
We launch paper boats into reluctant
space, speak of containment as if it were a
plan. Your last avowal has left
the station. There you stand without
 a witness, consigned to speak.

Written

Light was not something that crossed emptiness.

John Berger

The story, written in leaves, is of distance and turning. How to exit by means of a season without the sharp folding of a paper notion? Reliquary and shadow box dance a brief tango to how we meant paint but simply said black. And acres are burning in driest September, goodbye to all that, a condition of matter. Say water and the box remains empty. Light beams on the surfeit.

Want

...a stage between bent and mistaken.

Rosmarie Waldrop

A painting carves the rescue and the
drowning, as lovers' arms reach for the story
you create to punish time. Distraction gray
and ghostly in pale November light, a moment
teases grief to sit beside you at the window
where darkness stains your face as fresco.
You forecast endings battered by your sight.
Please, wind, be merciful to what margins
the sum of the morning leaves.

Museum

The train trains on.

Ann Lauterbach

Oblivion assured, you take the ramp that leads to evidence:
two lefts before the turn, a museum is refracted
with plaques reading *forgiveness, mercy, recondite,*
witness, you who were window and shade
in the long-shadowed garden, where no one
hung his hat on a branch or blistered sepia with a face.
We barter our habits, make questions fill reckless days,
page erased by a trickle of rain. It is evening and evening again.

Acknowledgments

Poems have appeared in the following journals in slightly different form; thanks and appreciation to the editors.

Conjunctions, Web Conjunctions, Plume, Poetry, Dusie Press Blog, Connotation Press: An Online Abstract, Jacar Press, Hambone, Ampersand Review, Blab, Undine, Airbrush, Volt, Free Verse, Lungfull, Brooklyn Rail, Cosmonaut Avenue, Negative Capability, Big Bridge, Landowich, Litscape, Intimacy, Truck, Columbia Poetry Review, Laurel Review, Fuzz, Blood Orange Review, Know Me Here (anthology), and Fifth Wednesday.

Subito Press Titles

2008

Little Red Riding Hood Missed the Bus by Kristin Abraham

With One's Own Eyes: Sherwood Anderson's Realities
by Sherwood Anderson
Edited and with an Introduction by Welford D. Taylor

My Untimely Death by Adam Peterson

Dear Professor, Do You Live in a Vacuum? by Nin Andrews

2009

Self-Titled Debut by Andrew Farkas

F-Stein by L.J. Moore

2010

Song & Glass by Stan Mir

Moon Is Cotton & She Laugh All Night by Tracy Debrincat

Bartleby, the Sportscaster by Ted Pelton

2011

The Body, The Rooms by Andy Frazee

Death-in-a-Box by Alta Ifland

Man Years by Sandra Doller

2012

We Have With Us Your Sky by Melanie Hubbard

Vs. Death Noises by Marcus Pactor

The Explosions by Mathias Svalina

2013

Because I Am the Sea I Want to Be the Shore by Renée Ashley

The Cucumber King of Kèdainiai by Wendell Mayo

Domestic Disturbances by Peter Grandbois

2014

Liner Notes by James Brubaker

As We Know by Amaranth Borsuk & Andy Finch

Letters & Buildings by Thomas Hummel

2016

New Animals by Nick Francis Potter

Sometimes We Walk With Our Nails Out by Sarah Bartlett

To Think of Her Writing Awash in Light by Linda Russo

Someone Took They Tongues. by Douglas Kearney

2017

Genevieves by Henry Hoke

Confessional Sci-fi: A Primer by Kirsten Kaschock

Sam's Teeth by Patrick Culliton

He Always Still Tastes Like Dynamite by Trevor Dodge

Anti-Face by Michael Nicoloff

A Forest Almost by Liz Countryman

Dear Enemy, by Jessica Alexander

Camera by Maxine Chernoff

About Subito Press

Subito Press is a non-profit literary publisher based in the Creative Writing Program of the Department of English at the University of Colorado at Boulder. Subito Press encourages and supports work that challenges already-accepted literary modes and devices.

Subito Press

Noah Eli Gordon, *director*
Ansley Clark
Laura Cordes
Mac Goad
Whitney Kerutis
Elizabeth Laughlin
Jessica Lawson
Hillary Susz
Kailey Alyssa
Rushi Vyas
Marcus Williams